DUGOUTS

DUGOUTS

David Bauckham

NEW HOLLAND

Foreword

It doesn't matter what dugout you're in, you still find yourself in the same situation.

From Non League grounds to Old Trafford, you are watching the game, weighing up the decisions you can make, hoping to change the game in your favour.

Up and down the country you get different views in different dugouts – and I've seen enough of them in my 15 years as a manager.

Some only offer a view of the players' legs, others will give you a comfortable seat. Some will pitch you in the middle of opposing fans while others can leave you in isolation. But there will always be the same decisions that have to be made.

How many games have been won or lost by a manager making a split-second decision in a dugout? And how do we know?

Different dugouts can witness contrasting emotions from week-to-week. The heart rates of some managers have been known to reach 197 beats-per-minute during the course of 90 minutes, whereas other managers can be calm and relaxed.

Some managers kick every ball in frustration, and there have been a few that have escaped the dugout by being banished to the stands!

Invariably, a whole week of work can come down to those 90 minutes in a dugout. Some decisions are made for managers, while others can be hailed as fantastic management.

One thing that is for sure, however, is that whatever changes take place in football – and we have had plenty of those over the years – there will always be the dugout.

Alan Curbishley

Notes from an expert

'Please do not swear', begs a notice painted on the back of the dugouts at Holmer Green FC near High Wycombe. A triumph of hope over experience if ever there was. Generations of football spectators have grown up in the full expectation that should the action ever flag on the field, or take a turn for the worse, the first place one looks to for a diversion is the dugout.

Today's managers are as much under the spotlight as any of the players, particularly in the Premiership. Their every gesture and facial tic tracked by camera lenses, they leap from the dugouts like excitable terriers, roused from their kennels at the merest whiff of a scrap. Or they lean against the dugout roofs affecting insouciance, or intelligent thought, or calm, when everyone knows they are praying.

In the same way that the minutiae of every 90 minutes is now picked over and analysed *ad nauseam* by media anxious to invest meaning into what is otherwise a pretty simple game (one 'ruined by the 22 players' as Danny Blanchflower caustically put it), so too we must now take heed of every precious little detail of the football experience. Hence we have been offered histories of the football boot, the confessions of a tea lady, surveys of meat pies, and even a dictionary of football slang, in which swearing is the least of it. I realise that with my record in publishing I must share some of the blame for this trend, a trend which, with this new opus on dugouts, now appears to have reached a new level of what some critics will no doubt dismiss as 'anorakdom'.

They may have a point. Or at least they would have if this were indeed a book simply about dugouts. But of course it is no such thing. The dugout of this book, as all true football fans will be aware, is a motif, no more, no less. In all its larch-lapped, creosoted simplicity, its breeze-block brutality or its ramshackle decay, it is symbolic of a sporting and cultural world that lies somewhere between the garden centre on the ring road and the working mens' club by the canal.

It speaks of make-do-and-mend. It turns its back on the hyped-up world of the superstadium, and, in several cases, cares so little for its surrounds that it blocks the view of the paying spectator. How stylish is that? Well, if a shed can win the Turner Prize, how about the dugout as conceptual art?

Some readers might spy here the influence of the documentary photographer, Martin Parr; champion of the boring postcard, chronicler of the mundane. They too may have a point. For which reason this book will be loved and loathed in equal measure. Because just like the obstinate, dedicated, track-suited souls who occupy the dugouts on matchdays, it cares not a hoot for the opinions of others.

Remember this as you turn its pages and delight in the unspoilt landscapes of British football's hinterland. The essential game, it would seem, does live on. No need to swear after all.

Simon Inglis

Introduction

Like many football fans I spent many years watching games in blissful ignorance of the humble dugout. Indeed it wasn't until I undertook to develop an online directory of all the Non League clubs in my home county of Sussex that I began to notice them at all. Even then, this wasn't the result of a deep-seated fascination, but the fact that at many grounds there wasn't anything else to take a photograph of.

When visiting an exhibition of an artist's work, it's often only when confronted with a sizeable body of that artist's paintings in a gallery that one really appreciates them. The same is true for dugouts, and I hope the photographs contained within the following pages will demonstrate the variety, subtleties and, dare I say it, absurdities that exist.

While the actual dugouts may not always be particularly awe-inspiring, I have also included examples that are nevertheless of interest by virtue of their surroundings. Whether rural or industrial, these are as varied as the dugouts themselves and provide a social and geographical backdrop for the so-called 'national game'.

Finally, I have also endeavoured to capture the essence of the Non League game in England and Wales. In some cases there is an air of nostalgia, but for the most part the photographs demonstrate the huge gap that exists between professional football; and the very lowest levels, which is experienced by the vast majority of footballers and coaching staff.

The author (right) impersonating a manager at Wick FC

I hope you enjoy this book as much as I have enjoyed researching and writing it.

For even more photographs of dugouts, grounds and images of Non League football, visit my website (www.pyramidpassion.co.uk).

David Bauckham

The Dugout defined

Look up the word 'dugout' in a dictionary and you will find any number of definitions. Similarly, the word means different things to different people. Ask a military historian and he will immediately think of protective fortifications, either constructed out of concrete or dug into the earth. However, even then there are variations. When does a dugout become a 'bunker' or conversely, a 'foxhole'?

Anthropologists will describe canoes hollowed out of tree trunks, and even dwellings. Dugouts as a means of providing shelter have certainly been in use around the world for centuries, particularly in regions with severe winters. Some of these dugouts were surprisingly well appointed. They had glazed windows, and properly hung doors. Quite often the dugouts were whitewashed inside and out, and there were lean-tos and verandas coming off the fronts.

In sport, the evolution of the dugout has occurred for similar reasons. Mention the word 'dugout' to any sports fan and he will immediately conjure up images of shelters on the touchline, used by players and coaching staff during a game.

In American baseball, the dugout is very much an integral part of the sport, and provides shelter for players of the batting side; whilst in cricket the comparison would be the far more genteel pavilion. The Association Football or rugby equivalent however, remains something of a Cinderella structure, frequently overshadowed by the more imposing features of a stadium, and unnoticed by most spectators. However, it could reasonably be argued that the dugout is one of the most important areas of all. Within its confines discussions take place and decisions are made that might change the course of a game. Before even the most basic shelter or seated stand is constructed, or even a perimeter rail is erected, there often has to be provision for a 'dugout' of some description.

In football there are surprisingly no regulations laid down for dugout design in the Laws of the Game. Whilst pitch dimensions, markings and even flag sizes are meticulously specified, there is no mention of the dugout.

The football dugout

In his book *Sightlines*, Simon Inglis relates how an open space can be transformed by the simple act of putting down some strategically placed jumpers as goalposts. Take this a step further by adding some marks on the ground and you have a football pitch. Add a perimeter rail and a football ground is created. In the summer months however, when the game takes a rest and wives and girlfriends rediscover their partners for about ninety days, many of these grounds disappear completely: posts are stored away, rails are removed and markings fade as cricket takes over many a recreation ground. In some cases though, the dugouts remain as sentinels to remind the casual visitor and dog walker of the important social function served by that area of land for a large proportion of the year.

The deeper one delves into the heart of the national game, the more basic these structures become until eventually they disappear altogether. Even then it is not at all uncommon to find portable dugouts, assembled or maneuvered into place on match days before disappearing from whence they came soon after the final whistle.

An important point to make is that dugouts are not all the same. Far from it. Forget the Chelseas and Manchester Uniteds; at Non League level, many clubs are run on a shoe-string, without funds to pay for building work, or apply for grants to develop their grounds. As a consequence many dugouts at this level of the game have been built by the club members themselves. Whilst they may not be great examples of engineering, such dugouts have been constructed by enthusiasts with a passion for their club and therefore have that all-important 'hand-built' quality to them. We are constantly led to believe that something that is 'homemade' is better and more desirable than something that is mass-produced. Every version will differ from its predecessor; it will be unique. The same applies to dugouts, although in some cases it has to be said that beauty is very much in the eye of the beholder.

Like those early inhabited shelters, some clubs take pride in the dugouts they have laboured over: painting them in the club colours for example, or emblazoning them with the club name. Dobwalls FC of the East Cornwall Premier League have the 'home' sign printed on the reverse of the dugout in their orange and black striped colours (pictured right). Now that's what I call attention to detail.

The materials used for construction also vary enormously, from bricks and concrete; to steel, corrugated iron and timber. Sadly, but inevitably, older dugouts are gradually being replaced by

Attention to detail at Dobwalls FC

pre-fabricated uPVC or perspex equivalents. With the odd exception, these have none of the character of their predecessors but equally, are weather-proof and not subject to the wear and tear of constantly being exposed to the elements.

The evolution of the football dugout
The first dugout in Britain, actually appeared in Scotland, at Aberdeen FC, in the early 1920s. Donald Colman, Aberdeen's trainer at the time, is generally credited with the idea.

Colman (pictured opposite) was certainly innovative while he was at the club and he was also a keen student of the game. During the close season he took up some coaching in Norway where, due to the climate, 'shelters' were the norm. It was from there that he is believed to have taken the idea for a dugout at Pittodrie.

Donald Colman in the first British dugout at Pittodrie

One advantage of sunken dugouts is that being so low, they rarely obstruct the view of the spectators behind. This may be true of the professional game, where finances exist to properly excavate the site and lay drainage, but is not always the case further down the football pyramid. Here dugouts are invariably at ground level and not always positioned in the best place: directly in front of the only area of covered spectator accommodation, for example.

Proper dugouts, sunk below ground level, are becoming less and less common, even at the new grounds of professional clubs. Some clubs have abandoned the traditional dugout altogether and have incorporated seating for playing and coaching staff into the main grandstand instead.

A further factor, and something of a romantic one, was that in addition to his footballing prowess, Colman was also a boxing and dancing enthusiast obsessed with his players' footwork. Because he also made meticulous notes during each game, and therefore needed a dry notebook, the addition of a sunken covered area on the touchline was doubly welcome. A few years later Everton visited, liked the idea and built one at Goodison Park. Don't forget that this was some forty years before the introduction of substitutes.

Sadly Colman's (and Britain's) first ever dugout has long since disappeared from Aberdeen's ground, although the current dugouts at Pittodrie are more or less exactly where the originals stood. The main stand was extended in 1928 and it is believed the original dugouts were still there at that point.

The most pragmatic reason is probably that sunken dugouts tend to become full of water, particularly during a typical British football season, and when the 'architect' has overlooked the important provision of a drain! However, it is equally true that it is virtually impossible to get a good view of the action from such a worm's eye view. Indeed many managers prefer to watch at least some of the game from the elevated grandstand. Here they are able to get a much better view of the action on the pitch and the tactics being employed by the opposition, while keeping in touch with the dugout below.

Ironically, Cambridge United's Abbey Stadium has a special VIP dugout where supporters can pay for the privilege of watching a game at ground level, before realizing that it is probably the worst view of a game they have had since watching their children kick a ball around at the local Rec on a Sunday morning.

Our American Cousins

Although generally accepted, the link between Donald Colman and Norway has never actually been confirmed and it has been suggested that a transatlantic connection may exist through the sport of baseball, and the baseball dugout in particular.

Credence for the suggestion that perhaps Colman may have been influenced by the provision of dugouts in baseball stems from the fact that the game was successfully introduced, albeit briefly, into Britain in the late nineteenth century.

Organised baseball came to Britain in 1890. That year saw the founding of the National Baseball League of Great Britain and Ireland. Despite this grandiose title there were just four clubs involved, and interestingly all had close links with football clubs: Derby County, Preston North End, Aston Villa and Stoke City. A primary instigator of the new league was Francis Ley, a Derby industrialist who had become interested in the game on business trips to the United States.

Ley had earlier developed a sports ground for employees of his foundry in the 1880s, and this became known as the Ley's baseball ground. Derby County FC made the ground its permanent home in 1895, and continued to play there until its demolition in 1997. By the outbreak of the Great War however, popularity of baseball had waned in Britain and whilst there may be a certain degree of logic in the suggestion, it is unlikely that dugouts actually existed at the baseball ground in those early days. Certainly, there appears to be no concrete evidence to support it.

As an aside, the evolution of the dugout in American baseball is certainly worth relating, and it perhaps has its origins in a game played on 15 April 1890 in Connecticut, by coincidence around the same time as Francis Ley was attempting to introduce the sport in Britain.

The New Haven Nine were hosting a game against the Rochester Hustlers and, after a bright start, an injury to the New Haven pitcher ended in a resounding win for the visitors. The home fans were incensed and, as the New Haven team walked dejectedly off the field, they was subjected to shouts of derision from the watching locals.

The following day manager Bull Burnham and his players were subjected to sustained criticism from sections of the crowd that were impossible to ignore by virtue of the fact that the bench was located directly in front of the grandstand. As the game ended Burnham informed the press that he wasn't going to expose his players to such ridicule for the entire season, stating that something was "darn sure" to be done.

At the next home game there was a long, red and white striped awning along first base. Behind it, and hidden from view, were the players; sitting on a bench that had been moved twenty feet away from the grandstand. It would seem that the 'dugout' had been born.

Substitutes

The evolution of the football dugout, and particularly its size, has parallels with the changing rules of the game itself.

It wasn't until the 1965/66 season that the English FA finally allowed the use of substitutes. Up until that time, if a player was injured he would have to carry on, or leave his side reduced to ten men. In those days, substitutions were ostensibly for injuries only, with the walking wounded left on for nuisance value, rather than for the tactical changes that are common today.

Keith Peacock of Charlton Athletic became the first player to be used as a substitute in England, replacing injured goalkeeper Mike Rose eleven minutes into a game against Bolton Wanderers on 21 August 1965.

From 1987 a maximum of two substitutions was allowed, before being increased once again to three, usually from a choice of five, although this may be up to a maximum of seven in some competitions. At the lower levels of the game however, many clubs do not have this number of players from which to choose. Despite this, it is not uncommon for a manager to name five substitutes on the team sheet, even if some of these are already injured and are not going to be used. To name less than a full complement of substitutes is considered a psychological advantage to the opposing team.

At the beginning of the 2004/05 season the FA made an amendment to Rule Three, which covers the number of players allowed, following their interpretation of a new directive from football's governing body, FIFA. In its amendment to Rule Three, the FA limited the number of substitutes in 'other matches', such as pre-season friendlies, to six. As is often the case with change, the amendment caused confusion, and outrage amongst some clubs, not least because the FA in fact does not make the Laws of the Game.

It wasn't long before the confusion came to a head, and the new season had yet to even get started. In a special commemorative pre-season game played to celebrate Fulham's return to their home at Craven Cottage, after a period as tenants at Queens Park Rangers, both teams had used six substitutes by half-time and the referee reminded them of the new ruling by the FA. In response the clubs claimed it was a breach of health and safety rules to make players play for ninety minutes, when they had only been in training for a week. Referee Peter Walton however, refused to be persuaded and abandoned the game. One of his Assistants took the whistle for the second half and at the end of the two 'forty five minute matches', the teams between them had used forty players. This created great consternation at the FA who immediately contacted FIFA, who replied that the decision restricting the number of substitutes permitted in friendly matches to six, referred only to matches involving national teams.

The effects of gradually increasing the number of substitutions allowed, and the number of players from which they may be chosen, has had a dramatic effect on the size of dugouts over the years. In the 2004 UEFA European Championships for example, no less than six team officials, plus twelve substitute players were allowed to sit on 'the bench'. If space allowed, a further five 'technical seats' were permitted, although there had to be at least five metres behind the benches.

Rules and regulations

As mentioned briefly earlier on, there are no regulations laid down for dugout design in the Laws of the Game. There are however strict guidelines on advertising that state, "There shall be no advertising of any kind within the technical area (the area immediately in front of the dugouts) or within one metre of the touchline and outside the field of play of the ground". However, this has not prevented clubs from placing advertising on the rear and roofs of their dugouts, which are perfectly positioned for such a purpose, often in front of the main stand. Even rules governing the technical area are not hard and fast, and the laws relate "particularly to matches played in stadia with a designated seating area for technical staff and substitutes". The FA accepts that technical areas may vary between stadia, and issues notes only for guidance.

In August 2003 Grays Athletic complained to the FA after losing an FA Cup tie at Sutton United. A penalty won the game for United, but Grays were unhappy and asked for Sutton to be removed from the competition as the dugouts were not equidistant from the half-way line. The problem had arisen after Sutton had moved the pitch following developments. Grays' appeal was unsuccessful and at the time of writing the dugout positions remain unchanged.

The fact is that, until fairly recently, teams have been able to do pretty much do what they like, although things are soon to change and Sutton, along with many other clubs will have to toe the line. As you climb the football pyramid, ground grading regulations come into play and they are increasingly affecting clubs even at the very lower levels.

At the beginning of the 2006/07 season, the Football Association implemented its National Ground Grading Document, which sets out what clubs must achieve if they wish to progress up the pyramid via promotion, or even retain their current status. Until then, regulations had varied between the various Leagues, and this had caused no end of confusion.

Perhaps the most bizarre case to highlight these inconsistencies came about as a dispute between Wealdstone, then of the Southern League and Watford of Division Two of the Football League, in the days when the Premiership and Championship were mere twinkles in a marketing executive's eye.

At the end of 1990/91 season, Wealdstone brokered a deal to share Watford's home at Vicarage Road. Prior to the building of the new Vicarage Road Stand in 1993 Watford's dugouts were still uncovered, after manager Graham Taylor famously promised that until the home fans were also under cover, he and his fellow occupants would suffer along with them. Taylor's players may have shared his altruism, although probably not! Nevertheless, whilst uncovered dugouts may have been acceptable to Taylor and the Football League, the Southern League did not agree and as a consquence Wealdstone had to purchase portable covered alternatives for their own use. Wealdstone ground-shared with Watford for two seasons before moving on to a new tenancy at Edgware Town, taking their dugouts with them.

The new regulations cover everything from ownership of a club's ground, quality of floodlights, seating capacity, number of turnstiles, press seating… and 'trainers' boxes' (the dugouts). At the highest levels of Non League football the regulations state that these must be clearly separated and marked 'home' and 'away'. Each 'box' must also be able to seat eleven persons, and that the technical areas must be clearly marked.

Even at Intermediate level, the regulations state that two covered, clearly marked 'trainers' benches' must be provided. These should be of equal distance either side of the halfway line, at least three metres apart and each should accommodate at least eight persons on fixed seats or benches. The saving grace here is the word 'should', rather than 'must'. Nevertheless, at this level, in some cases the seating for playing staff may exceed the actual attendance for the match itself. The requirement for fixed seating will also be a problem for those clubs that simply place a few chairs in the otherwise empty dugout. Even at the top of the Non League Pyramid, few dugouts had a capacity of eleven at the time of writing.

Such grading criteria are the principal reasons for the oddities in dugouts around the UK, some of which have clearly been extended or supplemented. Thus it is not that uncommon to find three or even four dugouts at a ground, sometimes on opposite sides of the playing area.

Some Leagues make the provision of dugouts a mandatory requirement whilst others do not, leading to some areas of the country that can only be described as 'dugout heaven'. Similarly there are other geographical variations. Shropshire for example, appears to have a preponderance of dugouts with doors. These are mainly for security reasons as they are used for storage; however the

Fortified dugouts at Plymstock United

massive steel doors on the dugouts at Plymstock United of the Devon County League are to keep out undesirable elements of the community.

Plymstock originally had pretty unremarkable dugouts, but being easily accessible they did attract the local youths who used to congregate in and around them. After a particularly amorous couple was spotted in one, there were calls for the dugouts to be demolished. In their place the local council generously provided the club with large, and very heavy, 'portable' dugouts, complete with handles and a trailer on which to transport them. When they came to the end of their useful life, the council agreed that the club could rebuild new permanent dugouts as long as they were secure – hence the massive steel doors (pictured above). If the doors look familiar, it is worth noting that Plymstock is not far from the Royal Navy base at Devonport.

Fortunately a modicum of common sense has prevailed with the proviso that portable (and somewhat lighter) 'trainers' boxes' may be used elsewhere as well, as long as they are securely fixed when in use.

Sometimes however, even secure fixing isn't enough. Bury Town of the Eastern Counties League have smart uPVC dugouts but during a game against Dereham Town on 20 March 2004 high winds caused much of the perimeter fence at their Ram Meadow ground to blow down. The spectators were moved to the main stand for safety reasons, but the players were not as fortunate, and the Bury substitutes had to take evasive action when the roof of the home dugout was lifted off by the wind. Eventually, both dugout roofs ripped off, despite the efforts of the Bury Directors to hold them on. A similar incident occurred at Southend Manor FC during the 1987 hurricane. The Chairman of the Essex Senior League clearly recalls seeing the club's two wooden dugouts being totally uprooted from the ground and literally flying over his head and away over Southchurch Park East, never to be seen again.

The future
As consistent ground grading regulations come into force and permeate down to the lower leagues it is inevitable that many existing dugouts will have to go. Indeed, by the time this book is published a number of those featured will have disappeared. Thus in some ways I am providing a historical record here. It's a sad fact that, like wooden grandstands before them, structures that provide many a Non League ground with a bit of character and individuality will be victims of a drive towards uniformity and compliance.

In many ways however, it is difficult to blame the clubs themselves. Wooden dugouts are all very well, but they do have to be looked after and it is not difficult to see the attraction of modern maintenance-free replacements. There is no shortage of companies willing to provide them either. There are however, a few clubs that are bucking the trend, although it is more likely that they lack the funds to do anything else or know a friendly bricklayer, rather than that they share my romantic ideals.

Meanwhile in the professional game, there appears to be a one-upmanship mentality with regards to dugouts, particularly at the highest levels. The Recaro company for example, previously best known for the seats it manufactures for high performance cars, has discovered a new niche for the provision of dugout seating. It would appear that the average multi-millionaire footballer is not content with having a superbly designed ergonomic seat in his Ferrari, he also wants one on the touchline as well.

Recaro have now provided seats in dugouts across the world, each set off nicely with the club crest or logo. Fans also want one, and seats are available in the club shop. What better than to wear a replica shirt with the name of your favourite player on the back, than to recline in a replica seat as well? Similar innovations have taken place at clubs from Sao Paulo to Real Madrid and, closer to home, at Newcastle United's St. James' Park Stadium.

The seating in Newcastle's new dugouts take the degree of luxury beyond even that enjoyed by the Real Madrid players at the Bernabau. The seats are specially adapted to help the players cope with the

State of the art dugout at Brøndby IF, complete with closed circuit television and luxury heated seating

temperatures of the North East in mid-winter, by the addition of an integral thermostatically controlled heating device (in the home dugout only I might add). Toon fans may pride themselves on being able to stand bare chested behind the goal at St. James' Park, but that clearly doesn't extend to the players. The contrast between the haves and have nots cannot be more perfectly illustrated by the players of Newcastle and their slightly less affluent counterparts at Northern League club Ryton FC, who have re-commissioned a couple of old bus shelters to use as their dugouts.

However, even the luxury that can be experienecd at St. James' Park pales into insignificance besides the developments at the ground of Danish club Brøndby IF (pictured above). Completed in October 2005, the Brøndby dugouts have embraced the Recaro comfort and the Capital Seating heating innovation, and taken the whole concept a step further. In front of each dugout a monitor house has been constructed to enable the coach to watch action replays, so at least he can confront the referee with an informed view in the event of a controversial decision.

Aberford Albion FC *(West Yorkshire League)*
Bunker's Hill, Main Street (South), Aberford, West Yorkshire

The village of Aberford is merely a goal kick away from the M1 and just twelve miles from Leeds, yet the football club's ground has a pleasant rural setting and a couple of smart wooden dugouts… even if the crowd never gets above double figures.

Abingdon Town FC *(Hellenic League)*
Culham Road, Abingdon, Oxfordshire

Abingdon Town are one of a large number of Non League clubs that at least attempt to make very ordinary dugouts appear a little more interesting. Painting the dugouts in the club colours is a common ploy, although adding potted plants is rather more unusual. However, it helps if someone actually waters them!

Alfreton Town FC *(Conference North)*
The Impact Arena, North Street, Alfreton, Derbyshire

Success on the pitch has resulted in Alfreton playing in four different leagues in as many years and successive promotions are reflected in the dugouts at the Impact Arena, as further seating has been required. Whereas accommodation for three substitutes was acceptable in the Northern Counties East League, new FA regulations state that in the Conference, there must be seating for eleven.

Altrincham FC *(Conference National)*
Moss Lane, Altrincham, Cheshire

Famous for their FA Cup exploits, Altrincham are one of a handful of truly 'iconic' Non League clubs and their splendid Moss Lane ground is very much a traditional football venue. One break from tradition, however, is the move away from pitch-side dugouts in favour of seated areas beneath the roof of the main stand.

Atherton Collieries FC *(North West Counties League)*
Alder Street, Atherton, Greater Manchester

The 'Colls' are by far the oldest of the three senior Atherton clubs, having been founded in 1916 by a group of miners representing the six pits within the district. When the pits were nationalised, the club was given to the people of the town. The well-worn but characterful ground has seen a number of additions in the last twenty years, but the rickety little stand behind the home dugout on the near side of the pitch has been described as leaning forward as if in prayer for its continued survival.

Aylestone Park Old Boys FC *(Leicestershire Senior League)*
Dorset Avenue, Fairfield Estate, Leicester, Leicestershire

Everybody has to start out somewhere, and a certain Gary Lineker began his career at Aylestone's Dorset Avenue ground, where these small but brightly painted dugouts adorn the touchline. The formative years of Leicester's favourite son are commemorated in the 'Lineker Lounge' at the Club.

Bickleigh FC *(Devon & Exeter League)*
Happy Meadow, Bickleigh near Tiverton, Devon

If there is a more appropriately named ground than 'Happy Meadow', I would love to visit it. Where else can you find an old barn and splendidly precarious-looking wooden dugouts complete with cushions?

Brixham United FC *(South Devon League)*
Wall Parc, Wall Park Road, Brixham, Devon

Holiday-makers at Pontin's Holiday Camp just down the road will miss out on a real treat if they fail to visit United's Wall Parc ground, with its wonderful double-decker wooden dugout, painted in the club colours and with spectator seating above. Not only does it afford a great view, but one can also eavesdrop on the conversations below.

Brodsworth Welfare FC *(Northern Counties East League)*
Welfare Ground, Woodlands, Brodsworth, Doncaster, South Yorkshire

Formed in 1912 as Brodsworth Miners Welfare, named after the local Brodsworth Main colliery, the club have played at the Welfare ground since 1924. The dugouts are unusual in having curved metal rear walls and also in that they are painted in different colours. The home dugout reflects the club's newer navy and white kit, whilst the away dugout (and rest of the ground) is in the old pale blue and yellow colours.

Brown Clee FC *(Shropshire County Premier League)*
Hall Meadow, Cleobury North, Shropshire

This 'dugout' looks just like a garden shed… and that is exactly what it once was. One of two rescued from the, now defunct, works team of the Star Aluminium Company in nearby Bridgnorth in 2002 and transplanted into this rural location, behind the village shop with sheep grazing in the adjacent field.

Broxbourne Borough V&E FC *(Spartan South Midlands League)*
Goffs Lane, Cheshunt, Hertfordshire

Borough's two enormous wooden dugouts, each with ten seats, complement two existing brick structures which on their own are more than adequate. Evidently the new dugouts have caused confusion amongst referees, some of whom have assumed that they are for the use of spectators, although the incorrectly marked technical area may have something to do with it! In case you were wondering, the 'V&E' stands for 'Victoria & Elms'.

Calne Town FC *(Western League)*
Bremhill View, Calne, Wiltshire

There are obvious advantages to having uPVC replacement dugouts, and the unusually tall examples at Bremhill View are rather smart. Ironically they are too small to meet new FA guidelines on capacity.

Chalfont St. Peter FC *(Isthmian League)*
Mill Meadow, Amersham Road, Chalfont St. Peter, Buckinghamshire

Colour coordinated seating conveys the club colours in the home dugout at Chalfont, albeit in need of a little attention... and perhaps giving a literal meaning to the popular chant of 'Who ate all the pies?'. Note the use of a car number plate for the 'home' sign: quite a common method of identification.

Chalfont Wasps FC *(Hellenic League)*
Crossleys, Bowstridge Lane, Chalfont St. Giles, Buckinghamshire

The dugouts at Crossleys aren't ideally positioned in front of the only area of cover for spectators, but since the club's record attendance is only 50 that probably isn't a problem. Some recent repair work is evident and is probably a consequence of vandalism: a perennial problem for clubs whose grounds allow open access to the public. Thankfully, the club has demonstrated good taste by not painting everything yellow and black.

Chelmsford City Youth FC
ECC Sports Ground, Fox Burrows Lane, Lordship Road, Writtle, Essex

Fox Burrows Lane is opposite Writtle Agricultural College and boasts these weird looking skeletal structures on the touchline that are hopefully covered with material of some description on match days.

Cockfield FC *(Crook & District League)*
Hazel Grove, Cockfield, County Durham

Visiting Hazel Grove today, with its large dugouts sited immediately in front of a pretty derelict cover, it's hard to imagine the club's glory days in the 1920s and '30s. The ground is, however, steeped in nostalgia. Christened the 'Village Wonder Team' after reaching the semi-finals of the Amateur Cup in 1922, Cockfield went one better and reached the Final in 1928 before being defeated 3-2 by holders Leyton in front of over 12,000 spectators at Ayresome Park.

Corfe Mullen United FC *(Dorset Senior League)*
The Admiralty, Mill Street, Corfe Mullen, Dorset

Despite being on the main A31 just to the west of Wimborne, it would be easy to miss Corfe Mullen's Admiralty ground, as it is hidden behind the South West Area HQ of the Clancy Docwra company. The big red gates are invariably closed except on match days, and it took several visits en route to the west country before I was able to gain access. The ground is railed but otherwise basic, except for a couple of bright red metal dugouts.

Crockenhill FC *(Kent County League)*
Wested Meadow, Eynesford Road, Crockenhill, Kent

Watching football amid the rural surroundings of Wested Meadow, it is hard to believe that Swanley and the M25 are only minutes away. The Crocks' boast that nothing at the ground has ever been built with the aid of a spirit level, and they are probably right. Below the bench there appears to be some form of heating device, but that is extremely unlikely… especially in the away dugout!

Darwen FC *(North West Counties League)*
The Anchor Ground, Anchor Road, Darwen, Lancashire

Darwen have a great history, having reached the semi-finals of the FA Cup in 1880-81. The 'Salmoners', nicknamed after their salmon and pink shirts at the time, were elected to the Football League in 1891, having been the first to introduce 'paid professionals' into the game in 1880. The Anchor Ground has been the club's home since 1899 and it looks as though the dugouts also belong to another age – the nuclear age. I am sure they could easily withstand the blast of an atomic bomb!

Earl's Colne FC *(Essex & Suffolk Border League)*
Green Farm Meadow, Halstead Road, Earl's Colne, Essex

Earl's Colne Football Club was founded in the 1870s and is therefore one of the oldest clubs in Essex. Green Farm Meadow has been the club's home since 1921. The brick-built cover, complete with a footballer weather vane, was built in 1999 and is flanked by two equally attractive dugouts each with pitched slate roofs. Smart and quite unusual.

Earlswood Town FC *(Midland Football Combination)*
Springbrook Farm, Malthouse Lane, Earlswood, West Midlands

Angled roofs at Earlswood's ground at Springbrook Farm. It *really is* a farm, and what this photograph doesn't show is the flock of sheep closing in on me after I disturbed their grazing on the pitch at this remarkably rural location near Solihull in the suburbs of Birmingham. I was aware of the bleating getting louder, and turned around to find myself surrounded. Very unnerving!

Eastbourne Borough FC *(Conference South)*
Priory Lane Stadium, Langney, Eastbourne, East Sussex

When it comes to dugout construction it certainly helps if your main sponsor is a double glazing manufacturer and one of your committee members is a bricklayer… but not when half of the seats collapse and have to be replaced with garden furniture.

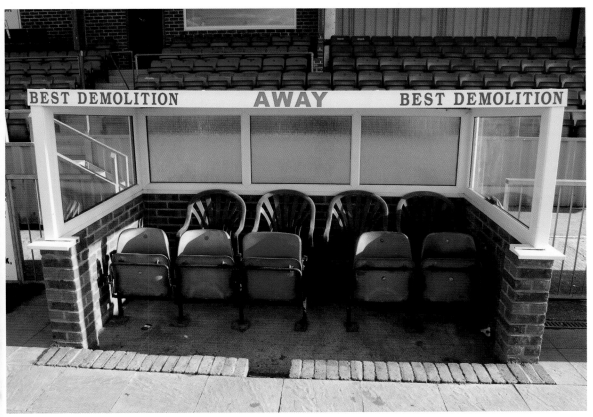

Eastbourne Town FC *(Sussex County League)*
The Saffrons, Compton Place Road, Eastbourne, East Sussex

The Saffrons has been home to Eastbourne Town since 1886, and is everything one would expect of Eastbourne; the Victorian splendour of the Town Hall and adjacent bowling club are fitting neighbours for the town's oldest football club. This is a case where the tourist office's slogan "The Sunshine Coast" was not appropriate, although amazingly this photo was taken in March!

Ellesmere Rangers FC *(West Midlands Regional League)*
Beech Grove, Ellesmere, Shropshire

Although dugouts with doors do exist elsewhere, they are particularly common in Shropshire where they are also used for storage and therefore need to be secure. Note the faded signs on the side, and the various dents in the metal cladded doors – presumably from being used as a goal by local youngsters.

Ely City FC *(Eastern Counties League)*
Unwin Sports Ground, Downham Road, Ely, Cambridgeshire

Ely may have moved from their wonderfully-named Paradise Ground in 1986 to newer facilities on the outskirts of the city, but one benefit of the move is the view of the Norman cathedral behind this smart brick-built dugout with ample seating arrangements.

Essex Police FC *(Essex Olympian League)*
Essex Police Sports Ground, Kingston Road, Springfield, Essex

Garden sheds aren't normally what one would associate with the police force, but the two coexist quite happily at the Essex Police sports ground.

Euxton Villa FC *(West Lancashire League)*
Jim Fowler Memorial Ground, Runshaw Hall Lane, Euxton, Chorley, Lancashire

It's not unheard of for someone to wake up and discover that their hubcaps have been stolen, or even the badge from their car; but the groundsman arrived at Euxton's rural Runshaw Hall Lane ground to find that the sign from the away dugout had been pinched. The finger of suspicion has been pointed at a rival club, and no doubt Euxton's players will be looking a little more closely at the visitors' dugout when playing away from home in future.

Fakenham Town FC *(Eastern Counties League)*
Clipbush Park, Clipbush Lane, Fakenham, Norfolk

The 'Ghosts' moved to their smart new home at Clipbush Park in 1996, and the ground is still being developed. In this photograph, Fakenham demonstrate a pragmatic approach typical of Non League clubs when faced with the problem of being two seats short in their dugouts.

Fareham Town FC *(Wessex League)*
Cams Alders, Palmerston Drive, Fareham, Hampshire

These metal dugouts on the far touchline at Cams Alders look for all the world as if they have been manufactured from a discarded container liberated from a cargo ship moored at the nearby Portsmouth dockyard.

Franklands Village FC *(formerly Sussex County League)*
Hardy Memorial Playing Field, Franklands Village, West Sussex

The Hardy Memorial Field had probably the most ridiculous 'dugouts' I have ever seen. They were little more than plywood partitions set into a flimsy metal cover that used to move from side to side. When Franklands Village decided to resign from the Sussex County League and relocate to a new ground in Cuckfield, the structure was swiftly demolished.

Great Yarmouth Town FC *(Eastern Counties League)*
Wellesey Recreation Ground, Wellesey Road, Great Yarmouth, Norfolk

Wellesey Road is a mecca for any serious grounds enthusiast by virtue of boasting the oldest surviving football grandstand in England, having been opened on 11 June 1892. The Victorian building is magnificent, but in front of it stand four small brick dugouts. The 'Bloaters' were refused permission to extend the existing structures or replace them to meet revised ground grading criteria and were therefore forced to build two more. As a consequence there are now two home and two away dugouts at the ground.

Guildford United FC *(Combined Counties League)*
Spectrum Leisure Centre, Parkway, Guildford, Surrey

Portable dugouts are invariably required at grounds that are primarily
used for athletics, and the Spectrum Leisure Centre is no exception.
In this photograph there appears to be a concerted effort to set a new
record for the number of people that can be squeezed into a dugout.

Halstead Town FC *(Eastern Counties League)*
Rosemary Lane, Broton Industrial Estate, Halstead, Essex

Another very good example of how smart uPVC dugouts can be. This is just big enough to accommodate three substitutes, Physiotherapist and Manager. Note the thoughtfully placed rubbish bin for players to deposit tapes, gum and empty Red Bull cans. The splendid main stand is a further reason to visit Halstead's Rosemary Lane ground.

Haverhill Rovers FC *(Eastern Counties League)*
Hamlet Croft, Haverhill, Suffolk

Rovers acknowledge that their simple brick dugouts aren't exactly the most capacious by providing park benches for the overspill at their attractive Hamlet Croft ground.

Heather Athletic FC *(Midland Football Combination)*
St. John's Park, Ravenstone Road, Heather, Leicestershire

One almost feels that 'Enter the Gladiators' should be played as the teams come out beneath this impressive gabled entrance between the dugouts at St. John's Park, immaculate home of Leicestershire club Heather Athletic (pronounced 'Heether').

Holman Sports Club FC *(Cornwall Combination League)*
Blaythorne Memorial Sports Ground, Pendarves Road, Camborne, Cornwall

These unusually tall dugouts are situated some way from the clubhouse at the Blaythorne Memorial Ground, on the far side of the cricket ground. I particularly like the hand-painted lettering.

Holmer Green FC *(Spartan South Midlands League)*
Watchet Lane, Holmer Green, High Wycombe, Buckinghamshire

When attendances struggle to reach triple figures, every word (and expletive) is clearly audible. Here, Holmer Green offer a gentle reminder to visiting opponents at their attractive, and very green, Watchet Lane ground. There is a further notice painted on the rear of the dugouts, politely asking people not to climb on them. Note the discarded Coke can on the bench.

Hopesgate United FC *(Shropshire County Premier League)*
The Cotes, Snailbeach, Shropshire

The Cotes is home to Hopesgate, on the edge of the tiny former lead mining village of Snailbeach high in the Stretton Hills, and lending a whole new meaning to the word 'remote'. There are two pitches, each with dugouts and on a fine day the scenery is stunning. Unfortunately my visit was accompanied by torrential rain, but these ramshackle dugouts were worth getting wet for.

Hurstpierpoint FC *(Sussex County League)*
Fairfield Recreation Ground, Cuckfield Road, Hurstpierpoint, West Sussex

These splendid portable dugouts are manhandled into their position on the far side of the pitch by the players before every match. Considering that they are stored in the pavilion a good 150 yards away that is no mean feat. This photograph was taken during the half-time interval of a match against Rustington.

Ivybridge Town FC *(Devon County League)*
Erme Valley, Ivybridge, Devon

Ivybridge's Erme Valley ground remains relatively undeveloped, but there
are two pitches, each with dugouts. Those on the first team pitch are
unremarkable, but these very low, austere structures on the pitch behind,
although not attractive by any means, are certainly a bit different.
Encountering them is a bit like setting foot on Easter Island and seeing
all those stone heads for the first time. Note the angled walls.

Lincoln United FC *(Northern Premier League)*
Ashby Avenue, Hatsholme, Lincoln, Lincolnshire

The press at United's ground in Ashby Avenue have no problem getting immediate post-match reactions from the respective managers – they just pop downstairs. I'm not sure whether the seats immediately below the press box are for Directors, or purely to cater for any overspill from the adjacent dugouts.

CPD Llanberis *(Welsh Alliance League)*
FFordd Padarn, Llanberis, Gwynedd

Previously known as Locomotive Llanberis when sponsored by the Snowdon railway, the ground at Llanberis has a spectacular setting and also dugouts on either side of the pitch with unusual wire mesh doors. Unlike similar dugouts in Shropshire with doors, these are clearly not used for storage... but to keep unwelcome visitors out. For non-Welsh speakers, 'CPD' stands for Clwb Pêl-droed, or 'Football Club'.

Loughborough FC *(Midland Football Combination)*
Derby Road, Loughborough, Leicestershire

Not to be confused with the more exotically named Loughborough Dynamo who compete in the Midland Alliance. This is the smarter of the two dugouts at Derby Road, which nevertheless look as though they would be more at home in a back garden with a swing attached.

Lyme Regis FC *(Perry Street League)*
Davey Fort, Charmouth Road, Lyme Regis, Dorset

Lyme Regis is best known as the setting for *The French Lieutenant's Woman* but Davey Fort, home to the local football club and on the cliffs overlooking the sea, is well worth a visit. A lovely venue for football in the summer, although I'm too sure about watching in mid-winter!

Market Drayton Town FC *(West Midlands Regional League)*
Greenfields Sports Club, Greenfield Lane, Market Drayton, Shropshire

The best time to photograph dugouts is soon after a match, when discarded tape, cans, water bottles and, in this case, stretchers provide evidence of recent activity. This rather nice wooden dugout is built into the fence surrounding the Greenfields Sports Ground. Clearly no-one was nominated as 'dugout monitor' for the last home game.

Nelson FC *(North West Counties League)*

Victoria Park, Lomeshaye Way, Nelson, Lancashire

A very northern scene (at least to a southerner), with terraced houses and a chimney forming a backdrop to the dugouts at Victoria Park. Formed in 1881, Nelson were founder members of Division Three (North) of the Football League, which they won the following season. When their old Seedhill ground was demolished to make way for the new M65 motorway, the Blues moved to Victoria Park, christened 'Little Wembley' by the locals.

North Kilworth FC *(Leicestershire Senior League)*
Rugby Road, North Kilworth, Lutterworth, Leicestershire

It's bad enough siting the dugouts immediately in front of the only area of spectator cover, but to build them actually *inside* the shelter is bizarre in the extreme.

Peacehaven & Telscombe FC *(Sussex County League)*
The Sports Park, Piddinghoe Avenue, Peacehaven, East Sussex

The Tye dominated the Sussex County League in the early 1990s but at the time of writing languish in Division 3. On a fine day their Piddinghoe Avenue ground affords superb views across the Sussex downland, but its exposed nature means that it is not quite as pleasant on a wet evening in mid-December.

Pease Pottage Village FC *(Sussex County League)*
Finches' Field, Pease Pottage, West Sussex

Having had to move their pitch due to overhead electrical cables to get into the Sussex County League, and then having to build a permanent covered area to stay in Division Two after winning promotion, only to be relegated; the last thing Pease Pottage really needed was for someone to sit on top of one of their dugouts!

Pelsall Villa FC *(West Midlands Regional League)*

The Bush Ground, Walsall Road, Heath End, Pelsall, West Midlands

Rather an unusual concrete dugout design, with hand-painted lettering at the Bush Ground, leafy home of the Walsall-based Villains.

Peterborough Northern Star FC *(United Counties League)*
Focus Youth Centre, Chestnut Avenue, Dogsthorpe, Peterborough, Cambridgeshire

The Club's recent name change from Eye United, reflects an earlier guise as Northern Star, formed as a village side in the early 1900s. There are three pitches at Chestnut Avenue, all with dugouts. However, the main playing area boasts probably the biggest Non League dugout anywhere with eight seats for each team, plus a further four for officials... and room for more if required.

Pilkington XXX FC *(Midland Combination League)*
Triplex Sports, Eckersall Road, King's Norton, Birmingham

The Pilkington Glass Company's Triplex Sports Ground in King's Norton
is the home of Pilkington XXX. Managers who complain about interfering
club directors would be well advised to steer clear, given the location of
the club officials' area between the opposing dugouts.

Plumpton Athletic FC *(Mid Sussex League)*
King George V Playing Fields, Plumpton, East Sussex

The village of Plumpton is better known for its racecourse, which gives rail travellers something to look at as they travel between Lewes and London. Were they to look out the window on the opposite side however, they will see Plumpton's ground, with these tiny dugouts beneath the trees on the far side.

CPD Porthmadog *(Welsh Premier League)*
Y Traeth, Porthmadog, Gwynedd

The dugouts at The Traeth are on either side of the ground following the instructions of former manager, Meilir Owen, who didn't fancy having the opposition manager a few yards away from him when talking tactics. Not only do the occupants of the away dugout on the far side have a long walk, but they also have to put up with the public address system immediately behind.

Roche AFC *(East Cornwall Premier League)*
Trezaise Road, Roche, Cornwall

You could be forgiven for assuming that this is a coastal setting. In fact Roche Rock is in former China Clay mining land in the heart of Cornwall, and has a tiny fifteenth century chapel at its summit. This was originally home to a hermit who never came down and was given provisions by the villagers. There are further dugouts on an adjacent pitch, affording an alternative view of the Rock behind.

Rottingdean Village FC *(Brighton & Hove District League)*
Falmer Road, Rottingdean, East Sussex

Undeniably one of the picturesque settings in Sussex, an added bonus on the outskirts of the historic village of Rottingdean is two sets of dugouts. The new wooden structures were built in 2005 and look across to their breezeblock predecessors, and the much older 'Beacon Mill' (erected in 1802) on the Downs behind.

St. Andrews FC *(Anglian Combination)*
Recreation Ground, Thorpe, Norwich, Norfolk

The portability of the wonderfully idiosyncratic dugouts at St. Andrews means that games can be played on a different pitch if the usual playing area is not fit for whatever reason (being churned up by joy riders, for example, on the day this photograph was taken). The dugouts are separated by a tiny portable wooden stand that really has to be seen to be believed.

St. Ives Town FC *(United Counties League)*
Westwood Road, St. Ives, Cambridgeshire

The Saints' Westwood Road ground is one of many where the visitor will find an odd number of dugouts. In this case the club was informed that its dugouts were too close together, necessitating the construction of a new one further along the touchline. Rather than demolish the 'offending' dugout, it has been retained for the use of officials.

Scarborough FC *(Conference National)*
The McCain Stadium, Seamer Road, Scarborough, North Yorkshire

For obvious reasons Scarborough's McCain Stadium is a headline writers delight and photographers couldn't believe their luck on one occasion when a sign went up telling supporters that the snack bar had run out of chips. Although a number of clubs now incorporate tiered seating for substitutes and coaching staff within the main stand, it is unusual to see such elevated dugouts actually on the touchline.

Sheringham FC *(Anglian Combination)*
Weybourne Road, Sheringham, Norfolk

The Shannocks' home in the town of Sheringham on the north Norfolk coast is rather hidden away behind the leisure centre and cricket ground, and it is gradually being developed. Two rather elaborate wooden dugouts stand along the near touchline, whilst there are plans for a seated stand in the near future.

Shipston Excelsior FC *(Midland Football Combination)*
Sports & Social Club, London Road, Shipston-on-Stour, Warwickshire

It would be difficult not to guess the club colours from this smart humbug-style paint job on the dugouts at Excelsior's London Road home. Note how much larger the home dugout is compared to that reserved for the visitors.

Sileby Town FC *(Leicestershire Senior League)*
Memorial Park, Seagrave Road, Sileby, Leicestershire

Very unusual shuttered dugouts on either side of the covered area at
Memorial Park. There are seats inside, although one imagines the dugouts
can also be used for storage. The presence of graffiti and damage to the rear
wall of the shelter suggests that the club's security measures are fully justified.

Stamford AFC *(Southern League)*
The Vic Couzens Stadium, Kettering Road, Stamford, Lincolnshire

There is barely any room for this dugout on its plinth at the Daniels' Kettering Road home, which is rather appropriate as the club's nickname is a reference to Britain's heaviest ever man Daniel Lambert, who is buried in the town. 'Fat Dan' weighed a mighty 52st 11lb and was a huge 9ft 4ins around his waist. He died aged 36 of a heart attack in a Stamford hotel whilst on a trip to the races.

Stanley United FC *(formerly Crook & District Football League)*
Hill Top Ground, High Road, Stanley Crook, County Durham

The name and address of Stanley's ground gives the visitor a clue of what to expect. The ground certainly commands good views, but that is nothing compared to the old house on the near touchline that houses the changing room and serves as a general congregation point. The dugouts that stand on either side are nothing out of the ordinary but there is surely nothing else like it in English football.

Stocksbridge Park Steels FC *(Northern Premier League)*
Bracken Moor Lane, Stocksbridge, Sheffield, South Yorkshire

Stocksbridge Park Steels was created in 1986 with the merger of Stocksbridge Works FC and another local club, Oxley Park Sports. The ground is shared with cricket and in order to meet grading requirements, the club have to erect a temporary fence to enclose it during the football season. The seating for the main stand came from Hillsborough, whilst a sign on its fascia proclaims "The Future in Metal". Note the carrying handle on the side of the wooden dugout.

Sturminster Marshall FC *(Dorset Senior League)*
Churchill Close, Sturminster Marshall, Wimborne, Dorset

Churchill Close is surely as close to village football as one can get, with the pitch surrounded by houses on what is essentially a large village green. The playing area is roped off on match days and the unique dugouts are pulled into position by tractor. They are not as old as they look and were a requirement following the club's promotion to the Dorset County League, from which it subsequently resigned.

Swindon Supermarine FC *(Southern League)*
Hunts Copse, Highworth Road, South Marston, Swindon, Wiltshire

The present club was formed in 1992 by the amalgamation of two Hellenic League clubs, Swindon Athletic and Supermarine, playing at the home of the latter club, although not on the current pitch. The ground has been developed as the new club has progressed and the dugouts demonstrate the Marine's compliance with new requirements for eleven seats, even if they are not all necessarily in the dugout.

Tadcaster Albion FC *(Northern Counties East League)*

The Park, Ings Lane, Tadcaster, West Yorkshire

The dugouts at The Brewers' Ings Lane ground may not win any prizes for their aesthetic beauty but are the pride and joy of Assistant Groundsman Geoff Gowlett, a typical Non League club stalwart who is at the ground on most days. The dugouts were built by Geoff after securing a deal with a local scaffolding company and are practical in the extreme. Despite the club nickname and there being no less than three major breweries in the town, none currently sponsor the Albion.

CPD Talysarn Celts *(Caernarfon & District Football League)*
Bryncelyn Road, Talysarn, Gwynedd

Another example of some of the superb settings in which football in the lower levels of the English, and in this case, Welsh Non League Pyramid is played. Here the Cwm Silyn mountain provides an awesome backdrop to these dugouts at the Celts ground, built on the site of an old slate tip in the village of Gloddfa Glai.

Tipton St. John FC *(Devon & Exeter League)*
Washbrook Meadows, Butts Road, Ottery St. Mary, Devon

Although they have their own ground, Tipton St. John's first team actually play on a pitch tucked away behind Ottery St. Mary's ground where I discovered this curiosity. It was apparently constructed in a day (can you tell?) and has a sink (but no water supply) in a tiny room behind. Substitutes can sit outside on a fine day.

Tiptree Heath FC *(Essex & Suffolk Border League)*
Sports Field, Colchester Road, Tiptree, Essex

The problem of lightweight dugouts that are not properly secured is clearly demonstrated in this photograph at Tiptree Heath. In fairness to the club, this was one of a couple of old dugouts on an adjacent pitch. Newer replacements of the same design and brightly painted in blue and lilac are, one hopes, firmly pegged down along the touchline of the main pitch.

Uckfield Town FC *(Sussex County League)*
Victoria Pleasure Grounds, New Town, Uckfield, East Sussex

These small 'nuclear bunker' style dugouts are set into the grass bank
that runs the length of one touchline at the Victoria Pleasure Grounds,
and from this angle they certainly look as though they extend deep
below the ground.

Upper Beeding FC *(Sussex County League)*
Memorial Playing Field, High Street, Upper Beeding, West Sussex

Unique hand-made dugouts in position at the Memorial Playing Field. Along with most of the perimeter rail, the dugouts are set up prior to kick-off and stored away again afterwards. Note the transportation trailer behind the dugout on the right. Although Beeding were competing in the Sussex County League as this book was going to press, their form of the past few seasons suggests they may not be for much longer.

Warminster Town FC *(Wiltshire League)*

Weymouth Street, Warminster, Wiltshire

A great view of the dugouts and surrounding countryside from Warminster's Weymouth Street ground, high above the town. Note the absence of any fixed seating – quite common amongst lower level clubs.

Wem Town FC *(Shropshire County Premier League)*
Butler Sports Centre, Wem, Shropshire

Of all the dugouts with doors that appear to set Shropshire apart from the rest of the country, these wooden examples at the Butler Sports Centre are my personal favourites, and date back to when the ground was not as secure as it is now. Apparently they are due to be replaced, which will be a shame.

HOME

Willenhall Town FC *(Southern League)*
Noose Lane, Willenhall, West Midlands

As ground grading criteria becomes increasingly stringent, one is likely to find an increasing number of dugouts that have clearly been extended, like this one at Noose Lane. It must be very lonely for the player banished to the far corner of the dugout.

Willington FC *(Wearside League)*
Hall Lane, Willington, County Durham

Willington FC is another Durham club with a formidable history, having beaten Bishop Auckland 4-0 in front of 88,000 spectators in the Amateur Cup Final at Wembley in 1950. Similarly, the handful of spectators that now watch games at Hall Lane is a far cry from the 10,000 that saw the club play Bromley in an FA Cup tie in 1953. Willington have also reached the first round of the FA Cup on three occasions, most recently holding Blackburn Rovers to a draw in 1973 although they lost the replay 6-0. That left hand wall looks a bit wobbly to me!

Wolverhampton Casuals FC *(West Midlands Regional League)*
Brinsford Stadium, Brinsford Lane, Coven Heath, Wolverhampton, West Midlands

Ivy adorns the dugouts at the Casuals' ground in Coven Heath, with their unusual suspended angled roofs. The numbers on the benches are not really visible in this picture, but betray a mysterious earlier use.

Acknowledgements

So many people have contributed to this book in some way, that it is difficult to list them all. However, I am particularly indebted to Colin Peel, who pointed me in the direction of clubs I never knew existed, let alone that they had dugouts worthy of interest. Also to Kevin Stirling, historian of Aberdeen FC, who not only provided me with valuable information about Donald Colman, but who also tracked down priceless photographs of the instigator of the British dugout without which this book would not be complete.

Dan Braddock also deserves a special mention for acting as my guide, chauffeur and umbrella holder during a particularly wet day in Shropshire. Similarly to Nigel Hammond who I followed around Leicestershire and kindred spirits such as Jon Weaver, Nick Mattlock, Vince Taylor and Steve Flinders. All have contributed excellent photographs, as has Mike Floate, a formative influence who also published my first book on Sussex Non League grounds. Finally, I must mention Simon Inglis who honoured me by agreeing to write the foreword for the book.

Not forgetting others who volunteered help, photographs and information to various degrees, even if it didn't eventually make it into print. If I have forgotten anyone, you know who you are.

Mike Amos, Freddy Berowski, David Baskwill, Bob Bluthardt, Terry Buckman, Paul Claydon, Gareth Davies, Nathan Davies, Robert Errington, Roy Fearnhead, Be Fretwell, Martin Gormley, Martin Harris, Peter Harris, Martin Haworth, Darren Holden, Dominic Horton, Nigel Hyde, Richard King, John Laidler, Peter Leavis, Tim Lees, Richard Lusmore, Hugh Mackinnon, Andy Medcalf, Joe Mock, David Miller, Richard Panter, Steve Parkinson, Ole Parmå (Brøndby IF), Dan Simpson, Andy Savage, Annegret Schmid (Recaro North America Inc.), Brian Smith, Brent Shyer, Roger Slater, Ray & Carol Stanton, Stephen Swann (Capital Seating & Vision), Uli Sudmann, Roger Taylor, Gavin Tutcher, Chris Ward and Martin Wray.

NOTE

This book was written during the 2005-06 season and therefore the information contained within does not take into account any subsequent promotions, relegations or restructuring of Leagues. Any other errors are entirely my fault.

94

David Bauckham p 6	Terry Buckman	Euxton Villa	Hugh Mackinnon	Scarborough	Dan Braddock
Donald Colman p 9		Fakenham Town		Sheringham	
Courtesy of Aberdeen Journals Library		Fareham Town		Shipston Excelsior	Colin Peel
Plymstock United p 13	David Baskwill	Franklands Village		Sileby Town	Nigel Hammond
Brøndby IF p 15	Flemming Alø	Great Yarmouth Town		Stamford	Dan Braddock
		Guildford United	Nick Mattlock	Stanley United	
Aberford Albion		Halstead Town		Stocksbridge Park Steels	
Abingdon Town	Dan Braddock	Haverhill Rovers		Sturminster Marshall	
Alfreton Town		Heather United		Swindon Supermarine	
Altrincham		Holman Sports Club		Tadcaster Albion	
Atherton Collieries		Holmer Green		Talysarn Celts	Mike Floate
Aylestone Park Old Boys		Hopesgate United		Tipton St. John	
Bickleigh	Steve Flinders	Hurstpierpoint		Tiptree Heath	Nick Mattlock
Brixham United		Ivybridge Town		Uckfield Town	
Brodsworth Welfare		Lincoln United	Mike Floate	Upper Beeding	
Brown Clee	Dan Braddock	Llanberis	Mike Floate	Warminster Town	
Broxbourne Borough V & E		Loughborough	Nigel Hammond	Wem Town	Dan Braddock
Calne Town		Lyme Regis		Willenhall Town	Dan Simpson
Chalfont St. Peter		Market Drayton Town	Dan Braddock	Willington	
Chalfont Wasps		Nelson		Wolverhampton Casuals	Dan Braddock
Chelmsford City Youth	Jon Weaver	North Kilworth	Nigel Hammond		
Cockfield		Peacehaven & Telscombe		Newcastle United p 96	
Corfe Mullen United		Pease Pottage Village		Courtesy of Capital Seating & Vision	
Crockenhill		Pelsall Villa	Dan Braddock		
Darwen		Peterborough Northern Star			
Earl's Colne		Pilkington XXX			
Earlswood Town		Plumpton Athletic			
Eastbourne Borough		Porthmadog	Mike Floate		
Eastbourne Town		Roche			
Ellesmere Rangers		Rottingdean Village			
Ely City		St. Andrews	Vince Taylor		
Essex Police	Martin Gormley	St. Ives Town			

95

Dedication

To the memory of Donald Colman, instigator of the dugout in British football and without whom this book might never have been written.

To my long-suffering wife Carina and son Jonathan, who have spent many hours waiting in car parks of football grounds during so-called 'family holidays' whilst I have salivated over yet another 'concrete box'.

96

First published in 2006 by
New Holland Publishers (UK) Ltd
London • Cape Town • Sydney • Auckland
www.newhollandpublishers.com

Garfield House
86–88 Edgware Road
London W2 2EA
United Kingdom

80 McKenzie Street
Cape Town 8001
South Africa

14 Aquatic Drive
Frenchs Forest
NSW 2086
Australia

218 Lake Road
Northcote
Auckland
New Zealand

10 9 8 7 6 5 4 3 2 1

ISBN 1 84537 478 9

Editor: Ruth Hamilton
Design: Paul Wright
Production: Hazel Kirkman
Editorial Direction: Rosemary Wilkinson

Reproduction by Modern Age Repro, Hong Kong
Printed and bound by Star Standard, Singapore